CELEBRITY BRANDING

THE ESSENTIALS, PROS, AND CONS

BY: SHAREEN KAHEAKU

Copyright © 2019

All right reserved. No portion of this book may be reproduced, stored in a retrieval system, or transmitted in any form or by any means – electronic, mechanical, recording or otherwise – except for brief quotation in printed reviews without the prior written permission of the publisher or the author.

DEDICATIONS

Dedicated to the ones I Love; To my two precious daughters and my lovely dogter. Mommy loves loves you all! To My Father who pushed me to take up photography as a hobby and who guided me to pursue my dreams.

To all of My friends, family and the Celebrities Worldwide, that I had the pleasure of photographing. Mahalo (Thank You) Talofa, Merci Beau Coup, Gracias, Salamat Po, Arigato Gozaimasu.

Table of Contents

- INTRODUCTION 5
- **CHAPTER ONE** 8
  - WHAT IS CELEBRITY BRANDING? 8
  - WHY USE CELEBRITIES? 12
- **CHAPTER TWO** 16
  - ESSENTIALS OF CELEBRITY BRANDING 16
    - SELECTING AN APPROPRIATE CELEBRITY: 17
    - EFFICACY OF CELEBRITY ENDORSEMENT 21
    - OTHER ESSENTIAL TIPS: 24
- **CHAPTER THREE** 25
  - PAID AND UNPAID ENDORSEMENTS 25
    - Paid Endorsement: 26
    - Unpaid Endorsement 28
- **CHAPTER FOUR** 30
  - THE PROS AND CONS 30
    - THE PROS: 31
    - THE CONS: 36
  - THE HUMAN FACTOR: 36
- CONCLUSION 41
- THE AUTHOR 43
- REFERENCE 47

INTRODUCTION

Be honest with me, do you feel intrigued by having your favorite celebrity come on television to run an ad for a brand? Do you develop some form of interest in the brand just because your heroic idol approves it as 'okay'?

Do you sometimes wonder why many companies are willing to spend fortunes, only to get a celebrity approve their products and services as "good and okay"?

In today's society, people are excited and obsessed with celebrities, like movie stars, musicians, athletes, etc. This obsession doesn't stop at the awe, they feel whenever they watch their favorite celebrities perform; it also extends to the celebrities' personality traits, their interests, and the ideas they represent, and whatnot.

As a celebrity photographer, I have witnessed first-hand the magical influence many superstars have on fans.

Many fans respect their favorite celebrities, enough to make them adopt their lifestyle and mannerism. Some idolize their superheroes and would fight and defend whatever their idols believe in, and would promote and uphold their values.

The celebrity-endorsed brand will elicit similar influence and effects from the target consumers when the idolized celebrity advertises the products and services.

Celebrity branding can be used across all mediums, including print, television, radio, and social media. Presenting a household name or a familiar face is the fastest way for companies to create brand associations in the minds of consumers. It does not have to be the big companies utilizing celebrity branding, nor does the celebrity have to be an international superstar.

As a business owner who is interested in celebrity endorsement, all you need to do is to identify and study the target population of consumers that your brand serves, and then choose an appropriate celebrity to match to your target consumers.

In my years as a small business owner and event promoter, I have utilized local celebrities in order to increase the growth of products and services that targeted the local population.

This book is not only for business owners; it will undoubtedly be useful for the celebrities that wish to go into an endorsement deals with companies. As a celebrity, this book will help you realize that endorsements are not about you, but what you stand for and bring to your brand.

The brand association that celebrities create in the mind of the consumers is the most important thing to the business owner. To achieve a splendid brand association for the consumers of your products and services, you will have to learn to use and apply certain principles to do this. In which this book offers to you on a platter. I hope you enjoy the read. Let's get started.

CHAPTER ONE
What is Celebrity Branding?

Celebrity branding also known as endorsement, is the promotion of products or services by a celebrity.

It is a type of a brand promotion that utilizing a famous person in marketing campaigns to advertise the product or service by using his or her fame and place in society (Keller, K. L. 2012).

Celebrity branding is a promotional tool that boosts brand awareness, enhances credibility, and gains visibility for brands. It is a marketing tactic featuring a famous person to offer an endorsement of a product. Most commonly, the companies which use this type of promotion are the fashion and perfumes manufacturers.

(Mentix, A. 2010), However, any business can employ the principles of celebrity endorsement for brand promotion.

Celebrity endorsements aim to rapidly increase the level of a company's public relations as it quickly attracts the attention of paparazzi and the media in general. One of the most invaluable techniques you can use to promote your product and services. Is the ability to have a Celebrity talk about your business.

For example; I had a friend who owned a food truck and his chow were always tasty and delicious. I used my influence to convince prominent personalities in the entertainment industry to try his food. They loved it, and publicly showered my friend's with rave reviews. The reviews did not only make my friend's food spot popular, but it increased his sales significantly.

Over the years, branding has transitioned from celebrities giving their express approval of a product. They are advertising to a more subtle approach, of emphasizing the benefits by the star, who are featured in carefully crafted storylines.

The main reason why a celebrity endorser may be particularly useful is that they make an advertisement stand out (Dean and Biswas, 2001). Research has illustrated that celebrities have a subtle, but effective impact on the everyday behavior and general lifestyle of individuals, as they tend to form an illusionary rapport with their idol.

In our current society, it has become a common phenomenon for celebrities to go beyond their usual trade and endorse products. Regardless of the enormous costs and risks involved, many marketers and business promoters still clamor for the endorsement of their brands by celebrities.

Studies have shown that celebrity endorsers can have a more positive effect on consumers' buying intention than non-celebrities (Byrne, Whitehead, & Breen, 2003). The rate of the relevance and demand for celebrity endorsement for a company's products and services appear to be on a rapid increase and don't seem like it will stop any time soon.

If conceptualized and used appropriately, celebrity branding can make an excellent and very viable marketing strategy. It can also provide the brand with a competitive advantage, and help build the brand's equity

Customers gravitate naturally towards patronizing products and services that have been endorsed by their favorite celebrity. As a result, they derive some fulfillment from using these products because they see the image of the celebrity in the brand. This is the reason why many big companies today have switched to the endorsement of their products by a well-known personality, trusting and believing it will help sell their goods and services.

Celebrities have a powerful influence over a significant number of people, and these people represent potential consumers of the brand to be endorsed. Also, they have a vast and stable social network. They can reach maas amounts of people through several media platforms such as television, social media, radio, etc. People easily support and subscribe to any trend, products and services that celebrities endorse.... talk about the celebrity effect!

Why Use Celebrities?

Celebrities are well-known people with the powerful to influence a large number of people. Celebrities have achieved and enjoy cult status amongst their legions of fans and have unprecedented amount of influencing power. With their star power and magnetic influence, celebrities can draw the attention of their fans to the brand they endorse and promote.

We created a clothing brand called 'Local Girlz Wear', with my partner whose target consumers were primarily the girls in my local Hawaiian community. We decided to use a local celebrities to boost awareness of our new clothing brand. Amongst these local stars were Fiji, Alan Arato (Starlight Entertainment), Ben Taaca (Tihati) who posed in a photo with a model wearing the 'Local Girlz Wear' clothing brand.

This single act of using celebrities to promote our brand helped tremendously to spread the news about our new clothing brand.

Celebrity branding infuses and is not limited to, credibility, acceptability, glamour and including the many good qualities that the celebrity represents, into a new brand, thereby making it stand out as UNIQUE.

Celebrity endorsement speeds up the sales of various products and services. By advertising a particular product or service on multiple social media platforms, the celebrity will have made the products and services visible to thousands of followers which represent the people and fans following the celebrity on these different platforms. .

Social media allows us of more of an in-depth insight into the personal and social lives of celebrities. Social media is mostly useful in reaching the younger generations. For example, imagine the attention a brand would receive when a celebrity's competitor claims that a particular kind of body lotion helps improve one's physical appearance. The celebrity's effect of being seen posing with the cream against their well ripped bare body will transform the brand into a highly demanded product in the market.

As a result, people naturally trust a recommendation from a famous and loved public figure. Leading to many brands clamoring to promote their products through celebrity advertisement. Most celebrity endorsements and marketing campaigns try to suggest that the star uses the product personally and enjoys it. Some will involve the celebrity in the image of the brand, relying solely on the celebrity's reputation rather than their outright endorsement to the brand.

On the other hand, there are newer brands that purchase fake fans 10,000 sometimes up to 100,000. They also purchase likes and views to get in to the game of Promotions. At first it may help boost their brand.

Eventually it catches up with them. The people who pay these guys/gals will soon realize that this brand has tricked them. This transaction will cost these business' plenty of money, due to low ticket sales and low customer turn outs. These types of practices makes clients, promoters and venues mistrust the brand and eventually lose faith in them all together. Celebs be aware of these types of new brands. They may woo the younger generation and some inexperienced promoters. Instagram and Facebook shuts down these types of brands accounts often. So if you hear of a brand that has been shut down after running seemingly successful campaigns or promos. It's due to the lack of real fan following and monetizing to those less experienced promoters.

CHAPTER TWO
Essentials of Celebrity Branding

Studies have shown that people are willing to pay up to 20 percent more for a product, depending on who endorses it, generating higher revenues for the company, (Rumschisky, 2009).

The effect of celebrity endorsements on the evaluation of products, demonstrates that celebrities influence their fans, have also been studied (Sliburyte, 2009; McNamara, 2009). Researchers found that much of this effect results from consumer's association between the celebrity and the endorsed object (Choi and Rifon, 2012; Till and Shimp, 1998).

The quest to enhance marketing via celebrity endorsement is a promising journey to embark on. It not only brings the company a lot of publicity and revenue, but could also bring about the company's demise if proper caution is not taken.

In this chapter, we shall discuss and study the principles and essential factors that are involved in endorsing celebrities. The essentials of celebrity endorsement are discussed here, under three main sub-topics:

- Selecting an appropriate celebrity
- Efficacy of Celebrity Endorsement
- Other Essential tips

Companies always proceed on endorsement deals with great care and caution as this could make or break the company's brand. They pay proper attention to these principles:

Selecting an Appropriate Celebrity
The choice of the perfect celebrity to endorse a brand could sometimes pose a difficult task to marketers. Aside from the grace and charming elegance that most

celebrities are revered for, there are many other considerations to ensure that the celebrity selected will yield productive results. These factors are critically evaluated to prevent the dangers of endorsements gone wrong:

***Fame**:*
This is the primary quality that qualifies one to be considered a celebrity. For endorsement purposes, stars must have a wide range of recognition, or at least with a defined specific group of people. The more popular a personality is, the better he or she is for business. Celebrities have an astounding number of following on social media, and this can translate into a larger target population of prospective consumers. With the multitude of fans following superstars like Selena Gomez, Cristiano Ronaldo, and Beyoncé on Instagram, their approval of a brand on Instagram would have a tremendously positive effect on sales. Such is the power of fame.

Longevity Of Endorsement Campaign:

In 1984, Nike teamed up with an iconic NBA star Michael Jordan to produce the Jordan brand, "Air Jordan". The endorsement has since proves to be quite successful a turbulent market in 2014. Good collaboration brought the brand back and strong in 2017 and is still doing excellent in the athletic wear market.

Consistency in the match between the endorser and the brand is vital in endorsement deals to establish a strong personality and identity rapport.

Acceptance Of Celebrity By Consumers:

It's not enough for a celebrity to be famous. They must be liked and respected by a considerable percentage of the general public, including the target consumers of the brand. Celebrities with histories of scandals or any negative press can be bad for business, whether the allegation was true or false. It could be a risky venture to go into an endorsement deal with such influential personalities, as the brand could suffer.

Celebrity-Brand Attribute Match:
This is in line with the principles discussed earlier. Companies should ensure that there is a good relationship between the brand being endorsed and the endorser so that the endorsements can effectively influence the consumers and appeal to them, creating a positive perception of the brand.

Timing:
Signing emerging, promising celebrities while some in their formative stages, can save companies some cost. This is advantageous because it could be a win-win situation for both the company and the new celebrity. In order to collaborate with such celebrities, companies should constantly be on the lookout.

Efficacy of Celebrity Endorsement

In order to have an effective and fruitful endorsement, companies may want to look out for some crucial qualities in the celebrity they wish to work with. These qualities will ensure sustained brand loyalty and brand association with the target consumers. The following attributes are essential in the celebrities in order for them to be considered in endorsing a company's brand.

The Celebrity's Credibility And Expertise:

Credibility refers to the confidence that the celebrity conveys to the public. Expertise is linked to the knowledge and experience that the endorser has on a certain subject, (Freire, 2010).

Trustworthiness, professionalism, and expertise are qualities that endear fans most to their idols. Such fans tend to share interests with their favorite celebrities. They want to be like them and do what they do. Celebrity's credibility is an outstanding quality that cannot be overlooked before signing an endorsement with them.

As celebrity endorsements act as an external cue that enable consumers to sift through the tremendous brand clutter in the market, the credibility factor of the celebrity greatly influences the acceptance with consumers, (Roll, 2019).

After a long cascade of investigations was finalized in the 2012 report by the United States Anti-Doping Agency, cyclist Lance Armstrong was found guilty of using illicit drugs. Nike did not hesitate to separate themselves from Armstrong as their endorser. As a result, he lost his credibility, and was deemed a liability that could potentially cost Nike mass revenue.

Celebrity's Attractiveness:
Celebrity attractiveness insists that an attractive endorser will have a positive impact on the endorsement.

The target audience appreciates a charming, good looking endorser, better than one who does not have appealing physical features, such as an athletic physique, competence, intellect, and an exciting lifestyle. Studies have shown that celebrities with qualities similar to the above mentioned have a higher chance of enhancing the memorability of the brand that they endorse.

Celebrity-Brand Meaning Transfer:

This concept emphasizes that some form of compatibility should exist between the endorser and the brand for a perfect match. The skills of the endorser must somehow be reflected in the brand or vice versa.

When the German carmaker Porsche signed the tennis player Maria Sharapova to be the face of its company for three years, the Porsche CEO Matthias Mueller had said *"Maria is the perfect choice. Her profile and charisma are an ideal fit for Porsche."*

Sharapova is **fast** on the tennis court, and so is Porsche on the road.

The success of the brand-celebrity collaboration heavily depends on the compatibility between the brand and the celebrity in terms of identity, personality, positioning in the market vis-à-vis competitors, and lifestyle, (Roll, 2019.)

OTHER ESSENTIAL TIPS:

Here are other important points companies should consider for successful endorsement marketing:

Avoid Controversial Celebrities:

Just as have been established and emphasized earlier, Celebrities that are vulnerable to scandals should be avoided. They are not good for your business.

CHAPTER THREE

Paid And Unpaid Endorsements

As previously explained, celebrity endorsement can take so many different forms, ranging from celebrities expressly approving a particular brand, to advertising a product or service, attending public relations events. Celebrities with unique voices can also do audio advertisements in the form of voice-overs. Celebrities interested in doing this type of advertisement, must have a distinct voice that can be easily recognized, like Vin Diesel, Samuel L. Jackson or Morgan Freeman.

In countries like India, celebrity endorsement has gone to a whole different level and assumed paramount importance as the public almost worships their celebrities. In such a country, celebrity endorsement would means everything to the big companies because any brand a beloved public figure endorses automatically becomes the people's choice. This kind of endorsement leaves the celebrities richer than one can imagine.

However, in some cases, companies do not necessarily have to pay celebrities that are endorsing their product. Inevitably, celebrities will still use their product due to brand loyalty.

Next you will learn more about paid and unpaid celebrity endorsements.

Paid Endorsement:

This is also known as overt endorsement. It involves a contract between a brand and a celebrity. Here, the celebrity is paid some mouthwatering sum of money to represent the brand in an advertising campaign. In paid endorsements, the company may give the celebrity some guidelines to adhere to, and this may involve some restraints to the celebrity's actions.

Paid endorsements include the following factors:

Advertisement:

The advertising media can consist of television, radio, billboards, or magazine posters, usually showing the celebrity doing or saying something to help boost the product's good image.

*P*ublic Relations Events:

Brands can use events to show off their endorser and make the public understand that the brand is closely associated with the celebrity. In such events, the photos of the celebrity are taken in the background with the conspicuous logos of the brand, or anything else that would create a stronger brand association in the minds of the target consumers.

Social Media:

Twitter, Facebook, and Instagram are fertile grounds for brand promotion through celebrity endorsement. Here, the brand targets several thousands of the celebrity's followers.

Celebrities have an extensive reach on these social media platforms, which is the main reason some brands would insist they use the platform to get across to their legion of fans. Ultimately, this means that large audiences are exposed to the influence of the celebrity and this, in turn, encourages positive purchasing behaviors towards the brand.

Unpaid Endorsement

This is also known as covert endorsement. Unlike paid endorsements, unpaid endorsements do not involve the brand paying the celebrity to advertise their products and services. Here, the celebrities wear the clothes to be advertised or enjoy the products and services of a particular brand just because they like the brand. This is referred to as free advertisement. However, upon realizing that a celebrity has interest in their brand, companies can now send free samples to the celebrity and encourage them to use the products, advertising them publically and or share on their social media fan pages. By so doing, celebrities are indirectly endorsing the brand.

The unpaid endorsement might appear to be all favorable for the brand, but it comes with some great downsides. Since there is not a contract, the brand can not state guidelines and restraints on the celebrity's actions. The brand has no control over the message the celebrity is passing while using the brand. They are at the mercy of the celebrity while marketing the brand.

CHAPTER FOUR
The Pros and Cons

Despite the positive aspects of endorsements, the use of celebrities in campaigns may or may not be effective (Misra and Beatty, 1990).

With all the fuss about social media and its burgeoning use as a medium of information dissemination, celebrities now relate with their multitude of fans on a one-on-one basis.

Celebrities are widely loved and trusted by their many fans that idolize, believe and trust them, and share in their interests. These stars can shine the spotlight on all types of businesses. This is one of the reasons celebrities are sought out by various companies to advertise their products or services.

In as little as a single tweet by a celebrity endorsing a brand, and the next day, the company is making millions.

But you know what they say about all that glamour and glitter? Example for a celebrity who gets the ring and her suitor publicly does it for the world to see. Every Woman wishes that her suitor would offer her an x amount of bling in the ring. Say he gives her a 5 Karat. This sets a precedence for others in the future. The next celebrity who does a public proposal, would have to be more glamorous and with a bigger Karat ring.

Join me as we take a quick look at the advantages (pros) and (cons) of celebrity branding.

THE PROS:

We are all very aware of the many good benefits of celebrity branding.

The use of celebrities as endorsers helps to humanize the brand. This creates a brand identity as consumers begin to relate the celebrities' characteristics with the brands, (Ambrose et al, 2014).

Manifiest Brand Awareness:

The powerful influence of a celebrity can do a lot of great things in the minds of the consumers, and will, in turn, transform even an unpopular brand into the most wanted product in the market. Companies take celebrity effect seriously, in regards to the brand association it creates, in the minds of it's consumers. Having a familiar face like a famous athlete, endorsing a company's product. For example, the endorsement of a particular brand of sneakers, will automatically influence the brand status. Sales will sky-rocket, and the company's revenue along as their success will increase in addition to that of the celebrity as well. Michael Jordan and Tiger Woods are prime examples of the successful transformation of the NIKE brand due to their endorsements.

Let's take a look at another example. You manufactured a hair growth cream, and a famous bearded celebrity in a commercial advertising that he uses the cream. First, your hair growth cream would immediately elicit the attention it's consumers. Especially those that had never heard of the product, and more people will get to know that product exists in the market.

Secondly, the celebrity effect will push many to try the product. Yes! Familiarity is what your brand needs to blossom in the market. I am sure you can imagine what the resultant effect of increased consumers' awareness of your brand would be an increase in sales!

Boosts Brand Trust, Credibility, and Power:
Celebrity branding gives the consumers the notion of, "If a celebrity can patronize the brand, it must be one of the best." The endorsement of the brand is an overly expressive narrative of how good the brand is, or can be as simple as the Celeb posing with the brand. Whichever way, consumers tend to trust the recommendations from people of high repute.

The approval and recommendation by the celebrity of the product automatically add credibility to the brand. In most cases, the brand isn't necessarily as authentic as the celebrity and the company claims. It could be just another brand in the market, but once it gains endorsement by a celebrity, the future of the brand and the company suddenly becomes bright.

Heightens Company's Profit:
It's easy to deduce the resultant effect of having a celebrity endorse a brand. First off, the 'Celebrity Effect' will cause the legions of fans to flood over the brand, and in a short time, the company will be counting its gains. Studies have shown that endorsement by celebrities triggers a significant increase in the sales of a product. Since Nike's endorsement deal by Michael Jordan, the 'Air Jordan' brand has brought in over $3 billion in revenue. Michael Jordan, on the other hand, still enjoys the lifetime partnership deal that still provides him a

considerable yearly income. As of 2015, he was reportedly making $100 million a year from royalties alone.

Serves As Promotional Tool:

As a company, how the general public views your brand is very vital as it determines largely whether or not you should stay in business. Celebrity branding attracts a large amount of attention from the general public. The media starts to talk about the celebrity and the new brand he/she has decided to endorse as well. The media's hype of the product is very good for business and will go a long way in increasing the company's sales. Companies that fail to promote their new brands with a popular face and name may continue to remain unknown and hidden in the shadows of other known brands.

Sustains Consumers' Remembrance of The Ad:

It is easier to recall advertisement that feature celebrities, than those that do not. Also, people are more likely to pay attention or watch television advertisements featuring their favorite celebrities. Running adverts for a brand using a well-known figure sends a long-lasting and robust message in the minds of the consumers.

Links Celebrity's Skill To The Brand

Here, the concept of transfer of meaning comes is examined. This concept emphasizes that "the success of the brand-celebrity collaboration heavily depends on the compatibility between the brand and the celebrity in terms of identity, personality, positioning in the market vis-à-vis competitors, and lifestyle. When brand signs on a celebrity, these are some of the compatibility factors that have to exist for the brand to leverage the maximum from that collaboration" (Roll, 2019).

Once the compatibility factors are fulfilled, the target consumers begin to relate more with the ads and are better convinced about the credibility of the brand.

THE CONS:

The Human Factor:
All those special attributes that make a celebrity stand out; those unique qualities they transfer to the brand; can either decline or disappear when the human factors comes into play. A celebrity involved in negative events may affect the image of the endorsed product (Louie et al., 2001). The impact of these events is directly reflected in the company's stock returns. Also, the greater the celebrity's perceived guilt in the episode, the higher will be the influence on their endorsement effectiveness (Carrillat et al., 2013; Louie et al., 2001)

An example of this is the Tiger Wood's scandal. In the wake of this scandal which involving Wood's multiple extramarital affairs, the shareholders of Nike lost a collective $5 - $12 billion dollars. Another example is the case of Kobe Bryant with Nutella and Sprite. These companies had parted ways with Kobe after he was indicted on charges of sexual assault.

Nothing lasts forever, and the same goes to the glamour the celebrities bring and add to brands. Whenever celebrity endorsement goes wrong, the brand is faced with the risk of losing a fortune.

Celebrity Endorsement Is Very Expensive:
The benefits of celebrity endorsement can be mouthwatering, but the cost of sealing the deal could be eye-watering. Companies pay millions of dollars for celebrity endorsement and it could be a risky venture if the company's revenue isn't healthy. Most times the celebrities have nothing to lose by signing a brand-endorsement deal.

Their only concern is to collect money after landing a deal. Some companies that lack the financial backing for celebrities, do not like to visit or entertain the idea of celebrity branding.

Overexposure of Celebrity:

Celebrities may take the alluring bait of accepting as many endorsements offer as possible. In a as much as it seems that nothing is wrong with this, it could, however, cause the trustworthiness and credibility of a celebrity to suffer. Due to the lucrative nature of endorsement deals, it's understandable why celebrities would want to endorse many brands.

When the celebrity endorses only one product, the endorsement is evaluated more positively, and respondents indicate a greater interest in buying the product (Mowen and Brown, 1981).

The more products that are endorsed by a single celebrity, the less effective the endorsement is to the brand (Kaikati, 1987).

The fans and consumers might interpret this as "the star going broke or grappling with financial difficulties, hence the need to grasp any available endorsement offer." This might affect the cost of the intended celebrity the endorsement he or she was meant to have.

Celebrity-Brand Mismatch:

Advertising campaigns create a link between the product and the celebrity, causing a transfer of meaning that can either be positive or negative to the product (Till and Shimp, 1998).

Sometimes the advertisements by celebrities do not always add that desired 'magical' celebrity effect to the brand. This could be because the skills of the celebrity do not in any way reflect what the brand stands for. This kind of mistake could put the company in some big financial troubles. Also for brands that a Promoter would provide in order to build himself up, no one would buy it due to the person endorsing the product. That type of brand could not use celebrity branding even I they wanted to. Pagebreak.....

CONCLUSION

The ultimate aim of celebrity branding is to draw attention to the company's brand, and either persuade or manipulate the target consumers into consuming the goods and services. More attention means more target consumers, and celebrities with their powerful influence have a large audience which adds to the target consumers. Hence speeding up sales and company profit.

Whether we like it or not, we live in a world that has been socially influenced by celebrities. Some people respect and revere, idolizing and placing them on a pedestal. Others get massively influenced by their superstar's lifestyle: always wanting to act like them, talk like them, or even dress like them. Celebrities are seen as role models to a significant number of people. So you can see why businesses clamor to have their brands endorsed by these superstars.

The choice of having a celebrity endorse a brand is not an entirely rosy adventure. It could undoubtedly put your company and your brand in the spotlight of the business world, and it could bring your business crashing down faster than you could ever imagine.

There is the need, therefore, to consider all the factors mentioned above before opting for celebrity branding!

If you do decide to make this a career choice, this book can help you to find your voice, build a mass movement and effectively become successful. Utilizing Key note speakers, influencer's , and artists has proven to help boost a brand. Now that you have the tools to help you to succeed, I wish you the best! Hope you enjoyed this book and Thank you! To your Success! Happy Branding!

pagebreak.....

The Author

Shareen Kaheaku is a Hawaiian writer and Event coordinator, born on the island of O'ahu, Hawaii. She is a single mother of 2, and a high-spirited deeply motivated Key Person of Influence who had been through the thick and thin of life and emerged successful.

She also authored: **"How I sustained myself by trading bud brownies-Gaining sustenance from your hemp harvest – (Making CBD Products)"**; How to Enforce Child Support- How to get CSEA to work for you and your family". "How I Became a Key Person of Influence." "KPI- Trade Secrets" -Guide to Success" and "Kidpreneur business guide"- "How to become a Kidpreneur"

She is currently running an **Online Mentoring Course: #KPI-OnlineMentoringCourse #SustainYourselfNow.**

She grew her business from scratch and had struck gold in her business enterprise. She is currently a consultant for experts, influencers, speakers, and small business, owners helping them to create and launch their online courses profitably in 60 days.

She is famous for her unrivaled knack and engagements in small business promotions, celebrity photography, professional networking, mastering the winning pitch, as well as event coordination.

She had joined the entertainment industry in 2009 working as an Emcee, a DJ/Karaoke Singer. Her relevance and fame in the industry had risen rapidly.

She has promoted several bands and artist. She has coordinated various events such as First Friday in Downtown and at Aloha Tower, She has collaborated with Sponsors & had personally sponsored the Maitai Rumble and Deejay Spin-off.

She is a well-traveled writer who had been to Johnston Island, Arizona, Utah, California, Canada and had lived and worked in Nevada for 13 years. She has also visited Belgium, France, and Algeria in North Africa

She is a strong-willed, determined mother who derives her motivation from her daughters. She currently lives in Honolulu with her daughter and a dogter. pagebreak....

REFERENCE

Ambroise, Laure; Pantin-Sohier, Gaëlle; Valette-Florence, Pierre; Albert, Noel (2014). "From endorsement to celebrity co-branding: Personality transfer". Journal of Brand Management. **21** (4): 273–285. doi:10.1057/bm.2014.7.

Biswas, D., Biswas, A. & Das, N. (2006), "The differential effects of celebrity and expert endorsements on consumer risk perceptions", Journal of Advertising, Vol. 35 No. 2, pp. 17- 31.

Bhasin, H. (2018). Celebrity branding. Retrieved 12 August 2019, from https://en.wikipedia.org/wiki/Celebrity_branding

Byrne, A., Whitehead, M., & Breen, S. (2003). The naked truth of celebrity endorsement. British Food Journal, 105(4/5), 288-296. http://dx.doi.org/10.1108/00070700310477086

Choi, S.M. and Rifon, N.J. (2012), "It is a match: the impact of congruence between celebrity image and consumer ideal self on endorsement effectiveness", *Psychology & Marketing*, Vol. 29 No. 9, pp. 639-650. [Links]

Keller, K. L. (2012). Strategic Brand Management. US: Second edition

Roy, K. (2019). ANALYZING THE IMPACT OF CELEBRITY ENDORSEMENT: GOODS VS SERVICES Retrieved 13 August 2019, from https://covenantprojects.wordpress.com/2019/01/23/the-impact-of-celebrity-endorsement-on-consumer-buying-behaviour-a-case-study-of-seven-up-bottling-company-plc-2/

McNamara, K. (2009), "Publicizing private lives: celebrities, image control and the reconfiguration of public space", *Social and Cultural Geography*, Vol. 10 No. 1, pp. 1-23. [Links]

Misra, S. and Beatty, S.E. (1990), "Celebrity spokesperson and brand congruence, an assessment of recall and affect", *Journal of Business Research*, Vol. 21 No. 2, pp. 159-173. [Links]

Mentix, A. (2010). Celebrities in Advertising Waste of Money, Says Study. Retrieved 06 02, 2013, from undercoverstrategist.com: http://www.undercoverstrategist.com/blog/celebritiesin-advertising-waste-of-money-says-study.html

Ohanian, R. (1991), "The impact of celebrity spokespersons' perceived image on consumers' intention to purchase", *Journal of Advertising Research*, Vol. 31 No. 1, pp. 46-54. [Links]

Olenski, S. (2018). Brands, Branding And Celebrities. Retrieved 12 August 2019, from https://www.forbes.com/sites/steveolenski/2018/04/02/brands-branding-and-celebrities/

Roll, M. (2019). Branding And Celebrity Endorsements - Martin Roll. Retrieved 11 August 2019, from https://martinroll.com/resources/articles/marketing/branding-and-celebrity-endorsements/

Rumschisky, A. (2009), "The value of using famous personalities in advertising communications: a quantitative analysis of prices for a fashionable product", available at: http://knowledge.wharton.upenn.edu/article/celebrity-advertising-what-is-the-roi/ (accessed 10 July 2014). [Links]

Sliburyte, L. (2009), "How can celebrities be used in advertising to the best advantage?", *World Academy of Science, Engineering and Technology*, Vol. 58 No. 2, pp. 934-939. [Links]

Till, B. and Shimp, T. (1998), "Endorsers in advertising: the case of negative celebrity information", *Journal of Advertising*, Vol. 27 No. 1, pp. 67-82. [Links]

www.ingramcontent.com/pod-product-compliance
Lightning Source LLC
Chambersburg PA
CBHW031502210526
45463CB00003B/1034